BOOK ANALYSIS

Written by Catherine Nelissen and Pauline Coullet

Translated by Rebecca Neal

AF131420

Nausea

by Jean-Paul Sartre

JEAN-PAUL SARTRE

- **Born in Paris in 1905.**
- **Died in Paris in 1980.**
- **Notable works:**
  - *Being and Nothingness* (1943), essay
  - *No Exit* (1944), play
  - *Existentialism and humanism* (1946), philosophical essay

Jean-Paul Sartre was a French writer and philosopher. He was born in Paris in 1905, and grew up in a cultivated, middle-class environment, which he described in *Words* (1963), an autobiographical account of his youth. He went on to study human sciences, sat the *agrégation*, a competitive teaching examination, in 1929, and met his future partner Simone de Beauvoir (French writer, 1908-1986). He became a philosophy teacher and published his novel *Nausea* (1938), which was positively received by critics.

One year later, Sartre was drafted into the army. He was taken prisoner, and joined the Resistance after his release. During this period, he wrote his first philosophical essay, *Being and Nothingness* (1943). Towards the end of the war, he met Albert Camus (French writer, 1913-1960) and worked with him on the newspaper *Combat*. Alongside his resistance activities, he wrote a series of literary texts in which he expounded on his philosophy and definition of literature, going from novels to plays. His most famous plays are *The*

Flies (1943) and *No Exit*.

After the Liberation, Sartre founded the literary and political review *Les Temps modernes* ("Modern Times"). His books were immensely successful, and he became the leader of the existentialist movement. In terms of politics, he moved closer to the Communist Party (although he did not join the party), and supported the National Liberation Front, which was seeking independence from France, during the Algerian War.

In 1964, he turned down the Nobel Prize in Literature because, in his view, the writer must "refuse to let himself be transformed into an institution". He never accepted prizes, as he felt that becoming an "institution" would restrict his freedom. He took part in the civil unrest in France in May 1968, and died in Paris in 1980.

NAUSEA

THE NOVEL OF EXISTENTIALISM

- **Genre:** philosophical novel
- **Reference edition:** Sartre, J.-P. (2000) *Nausea*. Trans. Baldick, R. London: Penguin.
- **1st edition:** 1938
- **Themes:** existentialism, strangeness, worldview, absurdity, society, art

Nausea is a philosophical novel by Jean-Paul Sartre which was first published in 1938. The book made Sartre famous and was met with unanimous acclaim in the literary world.

Nausea took eight years to write and lays out Sartre's existentialist philosophy in the form of a fictional diary. As the days go by, Antoine Roquentin, the narrator and protagonist of the novel, writes about the feeling of strangeness and powerlessness that overwhelms him in the face of an existence which he discovers to be useless and irrational. He feels like he is unnecessary in a world which makes him feel nauseous, where everything happens without reason or need and simply exists. In this book, Sartre rejects received wisdom and argues that existence precedes essence.

SUMMARY

In Bouville (French for "Mudtown"), a small fictional town which brings to mind Le Havre, Antoine Roquentin, a solitary young man, is writing a biography of the Marquis de Rollebon, an 18th-century aristocrat. Antoine had previously left Bouville to travel. He wandered across Central Europe, North Africa and the Middle East before returning to his hometown, tired of what he believed to be adventure. For the past three years, he has been leading an isolated intellectual existence: he is a man of independent means, and has the opportunity to observe the world and pay attention to the slightest things in his surroundings.

One day, Antoine has an experience which both shocks and fascinates him: all of a sudden, the world becomes unfamiliar to him. When he picks up a pebble on the beach, he becomes aware that things, or at least his perception of things, have changed. He has the feeling that objects have suddenly taken on a life of their own. They are touching him rather than the other way around. Is this new outlook on the world a revelation or a bout of madness? In order to understand what is happening to him, Antoine begins a diary, which he gives the title *Nausea*. In this notebook, he gives an uneven and fragmented account of his experiences, no matter how trivial, as well as his fears and questioning:

> "The odd thing is that I am not at all prepared to consider myself insane, and indeed I can see quite clearly that I am not: all these changes concern objects. At least, that is what I'd like to be sure about. [...] Perhaps it was a slight attack of

insanity after all."

At the library, he finds himself unable to write his historical book: how can he write about something that has already happened? Outside, he tells the reader about his feeling of being brushed by a piece of paper which he picks up and his impression of "a sort of nausea" that washes over him when he feels the smallest objects existing. He soon experiences this feeling of strangeness with people too. One afternoon, he does not recognise himself when he looks in the mirror. He is frightened and goes to a café, which is the only place where he can relax and feel good: there, he becomes part of an anonymous crowd, while noise and alcohol insulate him from the strangeness of the outside world.

The attraction that these new phenomena hold for him is stronger than anything else. He abandons his historical book, which he no longer sees the point of, to devote all his energy to observing his surroundings. He no longer goes to the library to work, but to watch the other people there. For example, he focuses on a man he nicknames the Autodidact, a grotesque notary's clerk who wants to read all the books in the library in alphabetical order. The Autodidact's humanism repulses him: when they are eating together, he cannot help forcefully telling him that the world is stupid and existence is useless because nobody is aware of the life of things or other people, or even of their own lives. The universe is absurd because its absolute law is gratuitous existence, devoid of sense: "Every existent is born without reason, prolongs itself out of weakness and dies by chance". When we become aware of this state of affairs, we are seized by a sort of nausea, which does not go away until we close our eyes again. Antoine's disgust at existence grows when, some time later, he witnesses the Autodidact being thrown out of the library: it turns out that the man had a weakness for young boys and had kept trying to stroke their hands.

Consequently, the gulf between Antoine and the rest of the world widens. The absurdity of people sickens him. The bourgeoisie parading themselves after church and at museums disgust him. He breaks away from society, allowing himself to wander freely, which makes him afraid and paranoid.

Antoine meets up with Anny, his friend and former partner, and realises that she is experiencing the same thing as him. However, she refuses to admit it. She rejects the truth because she is frightened by what they have both discovered. According to Antoine, she is no longer living, but surviving. Their separation is inevitable. After Anny leaves for England, he decides to move to Paris for a time. Before he leaves Bouville, he listens to his favourite song, *Some of These Days*, in a café, and it makes him want to create a work of art, which he thinks is the only way to escape nausea and correctly understand reality. He then decides to write a novel, an adventure that would "make people ashamed of their existence":

> "Not a history book, because that is about what has existed [...] Another kind of book, I don't quite know which kind – but you would have to guess, behind the printed word [...] something which didn't exist, which was above existence [...]

> The sort of story, for example, which could never happen, an adventure."

Antoine thinks that writing this book will allow him to remember his life without disgust and come to accept it. *Nausea* closes with this reflection, as night is falling outside the café.

CHARACTER STUDY

ANTOINE ROQUENTIN

Antoine Roquentin is the novel's narrator and main character. *Nausea* is his diary, the notebook in which he writes about his experiences and feelings. Antoine, who is about 35, is an isolated intellectual, immersed first of all in his writing and then in observation. After spending several years travelling and chasing adventure in Indochina, he decides to return to his home country, France. When he goes back to Bouville, he throws himself into writing his book about the Marquis de Rollebon. However, he quickly understands that this text is of no importance, because all it does is talk about the existence of a man, when existence is inherently unjustifiable: all men exist without reason. He comes to this realisation thanks to a series of events he has seen and experienced:

- A pebble he picks up on the beach seems to him to be moving by itself. In his view, it is the pebble which touches the hand of the person who bends down to pick it up and not the other way around.
- A piece of paper brushes him when he picks it up, as though the intention came from it and not from him.
- He can no longer remember the name of a root which he observes for a long time. He tries to give it a name, but is no longer able to.
- His own reflection in the mirror seems strange to him. It is not him, but an animated image of his own existence.

Antoine is overcome by nausea because the world is becoming strange to him, and he initially thinks that he is going mad. He then understands that existence precedes essence: he simply exists, in the same way that things exist, for no reason. It is later on that he defines himself through his choices and his subjectivity. People are not aware of their own existence, or that of other people. They live stupid and superficial lives, remaining wilfully blind their surroundings so that they do not have to experience this unpleasant feeling. Otherwise, their uselessness and absurdity would scare them. Having realised this, he understands that only art allows us to reach a pure and soothing truth, by talking not about what exists, but about what does not exist and is merely fiction. He then decides to abandon his biography of Rollebon to dedicate himself to a novel.

THE AUTODIDACT

The Autodidact is a notary's clerk who spends most of his time in the Bouville library. He is a keen reader, and has given himself the immense, absurd task of devouring all the books in the library by working through them in alphabetical order. The fact that he is always in the place where Antoine carries out the research for his book draws the narrator's attention to him. Antoine puts his work to one side to focus on observing this strange character. According to him, the Autodidact is characterised by:

- **His general absurdity.** He illustrates the absurd side of existence with his extreme reading plan and his uncontrollable need to spend all his time at the library, but also with his outlook on people. Antoine think that his humanism is laughable.

- **His humanism and naivety.** The Autodidact professes kindness and goodwill towards other people, who are nicknamed "the Bastards" by Antoine.
- **His hypocrisy, since his humanism and naivety are ultimately only a façade.** His actions reveal far less noble intentions, given that he is banned from the library because he is a paedophile.
- **His compulsive need to learn.** This is the thing that he holds dearest, but it is taken away from him when he is banned from the library.

ANNY

Anny is both a good friend of Antoine's and his ex-partner. When he meets her in Bouville, he thinks that they will get back together, but soon sees that this is not going to happen. She rejects him just as she rejects their shared realisation. She wants to shake off the nausea that has overcome her in the face of a futile existence and a strange world at all costs. She lives in darkness, with her eyes closed to the reality of the world: she merely survives, afraid of what she has seen. She laughs in Antoine's face before shutting the door on him and leaving him for good to go to England.

THE MARQUIS DE ROLLEBON

The Marquis de Rollebon is a mysterious (and fictional) aristocrat who took part in French political life during and after the Revolution, in the 18th century. He does not have a real part in the plot, but has a key role in both Sartre's novel and Antoine's life. Antoine is researching him because he wants to write a biography of him. This forces him to spend most of his time at the library in order to find enough information to piece together the Marquis' life. However, he realises that cannot grasp who Rollebon really was. Even worse, Antoine realises that his attempts to pin the Marquis down serve only to justify his own existence: "Monsieur de Rollebon was my partner: he needed me in order to be and I needed him in order not to feel my being". His interpretation says more about the historian than his subject: by putting forward hypotheses about the Marquis' life, Antoine reveals his own way of thinking and acting rather than that of Rollebon. He will never know who the Marquis really was because he is not there to tell him.

Antoine embarked on this work to give meaning to his empty life, but he realises now that he has made a mistake. Since the Marquis belongs to the past, he no longer exists: "My past is dead, Monsieur de Rollebon is dead". By rejecting the Marquis, Antoine rejects attachment to the past. He then comes to understand that only the present matters. The Marquis de Rollebon therefore plays a part in his existentialist realisation.

ANALYSIS

EXISTENCE PRECEDES ESSENCE

Sartre's existentialism is forcefully expressed in *Nausea*. The author asserts that existence precedes essence: man exists before being, because everything exists and is created without reason. It is up to each person to determine their essence (meaning what they are) afterwards through their actions. While existence has a gloomy and negative side because of its artificiality and the horror that overcomes anyone who realises this, essence is linked to a sort of purifying elevation that makes each person different. For Sartre, existence and essence are therefore two opposing concepts: existence mainly concerns the material, the primitive and the general, while essence is immaterial and makes every person a distinct unit.

EXISTENTIALISM

Existentialism is a philosophy which focuses on human existence.

Existentialist philosophy emerged during the 1930s, influenced in particular by the theories of Kierkegaard (Danish writer and philosopher, 1813-1855), who was the first person to describe himself as an existentialist. He explained that the meaning of existence could be found in the vocation of every individual. Each person must find their own truth. Existentialism rose to prominence in the aftermath of the Second World

War (1939-1945), when people were beginning to ask questions about man and his existence.

Sartre was the main representative of existentialism in France. According to him, "existence precedes essence", meaning that man exists for no reason; his essence is not determined by God. Man defines his own existence through his actions and choices. He is therefore a completely free being, master of his own actions and destiny ('Existentialisme' in *Encylopédie Universalis*).

Antoine becomes aware of the existence of the world when he perceives a dead snake which exists in its own right in a simple tree root. Existence is this simple state of being there. Antoine conceives of it in its most concrete and unpleasant sense, and compares the root which exists to something slimy and sinister: a snake. He associates his realisation with a fall, a discovery of hell on Earth. Conversely, when he listens to his favourite jazz song at the end of the novel, he reaches the immaterial and soothing sphere of music: the melody does not exist, it is.

> "It does not exist. It is even irritating in its non-existence; if I were to get up, if I were to snatch that record from the turn-table which is holding it and if I were to break it in two, I wouldn't reach it. It is beyond [...] Through layers and layers of existence, it unveils itself, slim and firm, and when you try to seize it you meet nothing but existents, you run up against existents devoid of meaning. [...] It does not exist, since it has nothing superfluous: it is all the rest which is

> superfluous in relation to it. It is."

Antoine's quest is nothing more or less than the desire to reach this immaterial sphere of essence. In the course of his reflections, he has constantly come up against this fear caused by the primitive existence which is shared by all things. By listening to this piece of music, he frees himself and understands that he must create his essence himself. He will reach it through art, which allows artists to detach themselves from material realities.

NAUSEA

Antoine Roquentin, the novel's main character, illustrates Sartre's existentialist philosophy in that he experiences nausea, which is the starting point for the author's reflection. Indeed, the reason Antoine starts a diary is so that he can get to the bottom of what is happening to him. An strange feeling of unease, nausea, seems to have taken hold of him recently. What appears to him as a sort of revelation is the result of a great deal of thought by Sartre: Antoine is therefore a manifesto of existentialism, since his inner turmoil allows him to question his own existence and the way it is defined.

Everything therefore starts with the feeling of disgust, which is directly linked to the perception of objects. However, this feeling does not come from Antoine himself: it is outside him, in the world. It is more of a revelation than a reaction by Antoine.

Normally, in the act of perception, an object presents itself to a subject before the subject evaluates the object. In *Nausea*, the subject-object relationship becomes reciprocal. The subject no longer imposes itself on a single object, but on several objects simultaneously; at the same time, several objects impose themselves on the subject. When Antoine becomes aware of the existence of things, he discovers the monstrous side of reality. For example, he observes a seat, which he suddenly sees as existing:

> "It stays what it is, with its red plush, thousands of little red paws in the air, all stiff, little dead paws. This huge belly turns upwards, bleeding, puffed up – bloated with all its dead paws, this belly floating in this box, in this grey sky, is not a seat. It could just as well be a dead donkey."

This disgust inspired in him by the sudden perception of the existence of objects is nausea.

Sartre connects the term "exist" with slimy, repulsive organic substances, which are generally connected to it. Antoine also becomes aware of his own existence. Gloomy, negative language is used to describe this repulsive and frightening feeling of being. In this way, the narrator sees parts of his body transform into creatures that can move independently:

> "I exist [...] I see my hand spread out on the table. It is alive – it is me. It opens, the fingers unfold and point. It is lying on its back. It shows me its fat under-belly. It looks like an animal upside down. The fingers are the paws."

In the same way, his thoughts appear to him in the form of a coil: "The body lives all by itself, once it has started. But when it comes to thought, it is I who continue it, I who unwind it". Thought is a "sort of painful rumination". Antoine feels the anguish of thinking, which appears as an unpleasant pain. Although he wants to "prevent myself from thinking", he is of course unable to do so:

> "I exist by what I think... and I can't prevent myself from thinking. At this very moment – this is terrible – if I exist, it is because I hate existing."

Here, Antoine takes Descartes' method of doubt ("I think, therefore I am") to its logical extreme: "I exist by what I think".

Nausea is therefore a sensation which comes from outside the body, from perception. It works its way into Antoine and makes him question his condition. It is a physical sensation which leads to philosophical reflection.

However, it seems that Roquentin also experiences a sensation that is in some way the opposite of this unease. For example, when he is in the café, music chases the disgust from his mind: "Nothing has changed and yet everything exists in a different way. I can't describe it; it's like the Nausea and yet it's just the opposite". This sensation is the feeling of adventure. The world is there for him and he is there for the world. In this state, it seems to him that everything has its place, like a logical sequence: "Each moment appears only to bring on the moments after". Consequently, it is naturally through art (music, but also writing) that Antoine will be able to set himself free.

SEPARATE GENRES

Novel or essay?

Nausea is a novel: as a philosopher, Sartre often used fiction, whether in the form of plays or novels, to transmit his ideas. In this way, his narrative depicts fictional characters, such as Antoine, Anny, the Autodidact and the Marquis de Rollebon, in a fictional situation. However, Sartre's book is closer to a story with a philosophical purpose than a novel.

The first title that Sartre suggested for *Nausea* was "Melancholia", after the famous engraving by Albrecht Dürer (German painter and engraver, 1471-1528), which depicts an allegory of melancholy. This title would have been well suited to the fictional form of Sartre's work, as it evokes the allegory: the expression of an idea through a metaphor and, therefore, through a fictional creation. However, his editor advised against this title, so Sartre gave his novel the title *Nausea*, which emphasises the existentialist theme of the book. The work is a philosophical meditation based on personal experience, namely the experience of nausea. The reader interprets Antoine's thoughts as though they were Sartre's thoughts and his experiences as philosophical arguments.

Simone de Beauvoir explained that Sartre's ambition with this novel was to "express metaphysical feelings and truths in literary form"[1] (*La Force de L'Âge*, 2013: 512). The author therefore uses the novel to set out his philosophy.

---

1. This quotation has been translated by BrightSummaries.com.

Furthermore, most of his writing is marked by shifts between analysis and fiction: for instance, his essay *Being and Nothingness* includes fictional examples, descriptions, scenes and characters. In the same way, *Nausea* contains Sartre's philosophical reflections, such as his thoughts about time:

> "[...] all of a sudden you feel that time is passing, that each moment leads to another moment, this one to yet another and so on; that each moment destroys itself and that it's no use trying to hold back [...] The feeling of adventure would simply be that of the irreversibility of time."

Nausea is therefore a philosophical novel. Furthermore, within the story itself, Antoine realises that he will not be able to tell the truth about the Marquis through a biography, but rather through a novel.

The diary

This novel is also distinctive because of its form: it is written as a diary. Antoine is frightened by what he sees as the manifestation of a mental illness and tries to analyse what is happening to him using his diary, which is written in the first person singular. Through this approach, Sartre wanted to make the diary seem real, and he included an editor's note at the start of the novel which explains that the sheets were found among Antoine Roquentin's papers and are being presented as they are. Then, in the first sheet, which is not dated, a tacit agreement is made – the narrator must try to describe precisely what he sees, without exaggerating or influencing the reader:

> "The best thing would be to write down everything that happens from day to day. To keep a diary in order to understand. To neglect no nuances or little details, even if they seem unimportant, and above all to classify them. [...] I think that is the danger of keeping a diary: you exaggerate everything, you are on the look-out, and you continually stretch the truth."

We can view this as a kind of autobiographical pact, where the author promises to be as honest as possible in his story. In this way, by accepting the pact, the reader agrees to believe that this is a true story.

The diary form is interesting, because it allows us to track the development of Antoine's "illness" and his reaction to it: he pins it down, gets used to it, struggles, thinks about it, and finally sets about writing. This also allows the creation of a certain degree of closeness between the reader and Antoine, since, by addressing himself, he directly shares his thoughts with the reader. However, this openness also gives the reader the opportunity to question Antoine's point of view and interpretation. Antoine himself takes a step back to look at his way of recounting events:

> "How could I have written this absurd, pompous sentence yesterday: 'I was alone, but I walked like a band of soldiers descending on a town.' I have no need to speak in flowery language. I am writing to understand certain circumstances. I must beware of literature. I must let my pen run on, without searching for words."

He does not think twice about criticising himself, because he wants to share his experience objectively. However, this is impossible. He tries to study himself: he tries to see himself as an object, but he is still a subject. This failed attempt at objectivity echoes his abandoned biography of the Marquis de Rollebon.

Antoine's work also has some similarities with the thesis. This is a very specific genre, because it is based on the total objectivity of its author. There is no room for individual style or aesthetic taste. It is therefore not the best medium to convey personality through writing. Later on, Antoine says "I would have been better off writing a novel about the Marquis de Rollebon". Indeed, he does not manage to write by bringing together information about the Marquis' life: the more documents he amasses, the less able he is to grasp the character:

> "This isn't for lack of documents [...] On the contrary, I have almost too many of these. What is lacking in all this testimony is firmness and consistency [...] they don't seem to concern the same person."

In this sense, the Autodidact, who methodically accumulates knowledge by reading books in alphabetical order, relates to this idea by taking it to the extreme: he needs to have amassed all the documentation before he can start writing.

Antoine then understands that he is not writing about the Marquis but about himself. Indeed, even though he is defending "reasonable hypotheses which take the facts into account", he is nonetheless "only too well aware that they come from me, that they are simply a way of unifying my own knowledge", which gives him "the impression of doing a work of pure imagination".

This plunges him into a depression which drives him to write his diary and, at the same time, question himself about the unpleasant sensation he is experiencing. Alongside this, he feels the strangeness of the world and learns through his biography that the past does not exist.

Consequently, for Antoine the diary is a way not only of freeing himself from nausea, but also of transitioning smoothly between the objectivity of a thesis and the freedom of a novel. First of all, Antoine tries in vain to write a biography. He then sets about writing a diary, before finally finding his salvation by planning to write a novel. This reflects Sartre's project, as he decided to write *Nausea* not as an essay but as a novel. Antoine, who is torn between the essay (the thesis), autobiography (the diary) and fiction (the novel), is therefore modelled on Sartre. The interwoven presence of novel, biography, autobiography and philosophical discourse is the only response to the nauseating encounter with existence. The novel is ultimately presented as desirable because it allows the writer to use the imaginary as a way of expressing their subjectivity:

> "But a time would have to come when the book would be written, would be behind me, and I think that a little of its light would fall over my past. Then, through it, I might be able to recall my life without repugnance."

Sartre therefore favours fiction to escape nausea and share his existentialist philosophy with the world.

This first novel met with a positive reception from the public and the press, although some critics found its ambiguous form, halfway between a novel and an essay, disconcerting. They criticised the coarseness of his vocabulary and the fact that he was popularising metaphysics. Conversely, others, such as Maurice Blanchot (French novelist and literary critic, 1907-2003), praised the depth of his analysis, which the author had no qualms about inserting into the drama of existence. *Nausea* was a resounding success and marked Sartre's entry onto the literary scene. It has since been translated into around 30 languages.

FURTHER REFLECTION

SOME QUESTIONS TO THINK ABOUT...

- Explain the novel's title.
- When does Antoine Roquentin become truly aware of the source of his nausea? What exactly does he understand?
- Give five examples of phenomena observed by the novel's protagonist which lead him to his conclusion about existence.
- What essential place does Sartre give to art? According to him, in what way does it possess a life-saving force?
- The novel takes the form of a diary. Does it follow a precise and verifiable chronology or is it based on temporal indeterminacy? Explain how the temporal system of the novel forms part of the author's philosophical reasoning.
- What psychological stages does the hero of the novel go through? Show how they follow the development of his philosophical thought.
- Should *Nausea* only be described as a philosophical novel? If so, justify why you think so. If not, what other genres is it linked to and why?
- Show how the author's style ties in with his philosophical reflection. Is it rigid and classical or spontaneous and fragmented?
- The semantic field of sensations is used extensively by Sartre in *Nausea*. Find two examples of the semantic presence of each of the five senses in the text.
- Name an existentialist writer who followed in Sartre's footsteps. Briefly explain the similarities and differences between their respective theories.

We want to hear from you!
Leave a comment on your online library
and share your favourite books on social media!

FURTHER READING

REFERENCE EDITION

- Sartre, J.-P. (2000) *Nausea*. Trans. Baldick, R. London: Penguin.

REFERENCE STUDIES

- Encylopédie Universalis. (No date) *Existentialisme*. [Online]. [Accessed 2 May 2017]. Available from: <http://www.universalis.fr/encyclopedie/existentialisme/>
- Sartre, J.-P. (1964) Sartre on the Nobel Prize. Trans. Howard, R. *The New York Review of Books*. [Online]. [Accessed 2 May 2017]. Available from: <http://www.nybooks.com/articles/1964/12/17/sartre-on-the-nobel-prize/>

MORE FROM BRIGHTSUMMARIES.COM

- Reading guide – *Dirty Hands* by Jean-Paul Sartre.
- Reading guide – *Existentialism and Humanism* by Jean-Paul Sartre.
- Reading guide – *No Exit* by Jean-Paul Sartre.

Bright ≡Summaries.com

More guides to rediscover your love of literature

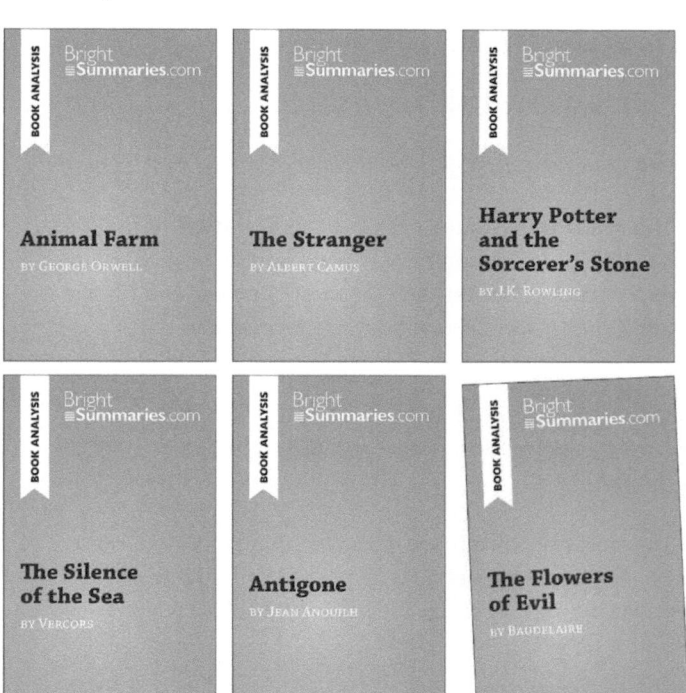

www.brightsummaries.com

www.brightsummaries.com

Ebook EAN: 9782806295798

Paperback EAN: 9782806297730

Legal Deposit: D/2017/12603/287

This guide was written with the collaboration of Pauline Coullet for the chapters 'Jean-Paul Sartre', 'The Marquis de Rollebon', 'Nausea' and 'Separate genres', and for the additional information about existentialism.

Cover: © Primento

Digital conception by Primento, the digital partner of publishers.

This guide was produced with the support of the *Service Général des Lettres et du Livre* of the Wallonia-Brussels Federation.